My Body

Paul Humphrey

Photography by Chris Fairclough

W

First published in 2005 by
Franklin Watts
338 Euston Road
London NW1 3BH

Franklin Watts Australia
Level 17/207 Kent Street
Sydney NSW 2000

ISBN: 978 0 7496 6185 4

Dewey classification number 612

A CIP catalogue record for this book is available
from the British Library.

Planning and production by Discovery Books Limited
Editor: Rachel Tisdale
Designer: Ian Winton
Photography: Chris Fairclough
Series advisors: Diana Bentley MA and Dee Reid MA,
Fellows of Oxford Brookes University

The author, packager and publisher would like to thank the following
people for their participation in this book: Ottilie and Auriel Austin-Baker;
Toby Frampton; Samiya Latif and Arrandeep Bola.

Printed in China

Franklin Watts is a division of Hachette Children's Books.

Contents

This is my body.

eye

ear

nose

mouth

teeth

4

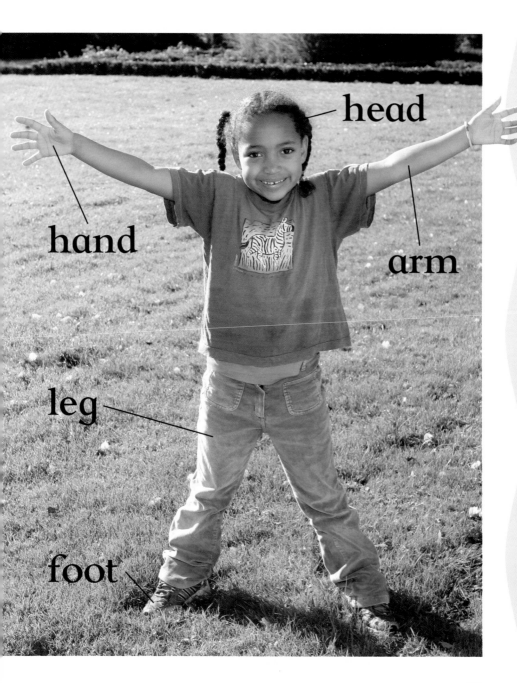

head

hand

arm

leg

foot

5

I use my
hands to beat
the drum.

I use my feet to kick the ball.

I can smell
the flower
with my
nose.

I can see the book
with my eyes.

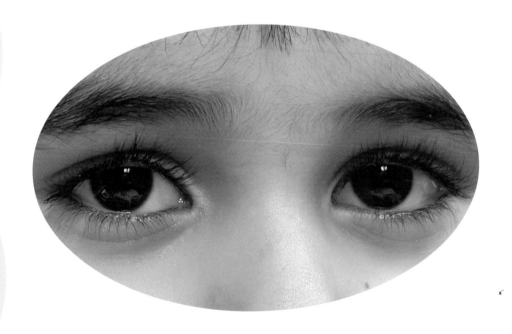

We talk with our mouths.

We listen with
our ears.

Our arms
are good for
climbing.

Our legs are good for jumping and running.

My teeth
can bite
the apple.

Our bodies are great!

Word bank

Look back for these words and pictures.

Arms

Ears

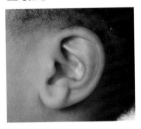

Eyes

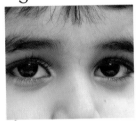

Feet

Hands

Legs

Mouths

Nose

Teeth